9 Ways to Nurture Your Marriage

William E. Rabior
and Susan C. Rabior

D1383648

Liguori

ONE LIGUORI DRIVE
LIGUORI MO 63057-9999

■ ■ ■ ■ ■

We dedicate this book to our daughter,
Gabrielle Rose Rabior.
We love you all the way up to the stars and back again.

We especially want to thank our editors, Susan O'Connor and
Kass Dotterweich, for the pleasure of their company on our
creative journey. The assistance they gave us was invaluable.

■ ■ ■ ■ ■

Imprimi Potest:
Richard Thibodeau, C.Ss.R.
Provincial, Denver Province
The Redemptorists

ISBN 0-7648-0585-1
Library of Congress Catalog Card Number: 99-67980

Liguori Publications, a nonprofit corporation, is an apostolate of the
Redemptorists. To learn more about the Redemptorists, visit
Redemptorists.com.

To order, call 1-800-325-9521
www.liguori.org

Cover design by Wendy Barnes

Contents

■ ■ ■ ■ ■

Blessing

■　■　■　■　■

May you be graced with God's presence
and gifted with God's grace.
May the Holy Spirit enlighten and enliven you,
and may the love of Christ sustain you.
Long after your wedding day is over,
may the days of your marriage be joyous and rich.
May you find shelter and safety in each other's arms,
respect and reverence in each other's eyes,
and a home in each other's heart.
May your friendship be faithful and firm,
your trust total.
And may you remain young at heart
as you grow old together.
May God bless you...and we do, too.
Amen

Introduction

■ ■ ■ ■ ■

This book came about through much talking—and even more listening. The idea originated in 1997, when we unscientifically began talking with happily married couples and with individuals who had been happily married but were now widowed about what they felt contributed to the satisfaction and fulfillment they experienced in marriage. The anecdotal material that we compiled was fascinating and, in some cases, not at all what we expected.

For example, we were surprised to hear so little talk about "love," although clearly the love these people had for their spouses ran deep. "God help you if love is all you have in a marriage," commented one woman who had been married for over sixty years. "You need more than that to make it work. Love alone may get you through the first year, but that's about all."

We also heard comments about the need for growth in marriage, that satisfying marriages are not static. "Marriage should be a verb, not a noun," one happily married husband told us. "It is something you either grow into or don't. So, for example, we should say that we have twenty-five years of successful marriaging and look forward to twenty-five more." And his wife heartily agreed: "Yes. Marriages don't stand still. If you are not growing *into* your marriage, chances are you are growing *out* of it."

If love is essential but not enough, what are other factors that contribute to a good marriage? How do we grow into a marriage so that successful "marriaging" does, in fact, occur?

As we started our search for the secrets of a successful marriage, we found that couples were eager to share their ideas and insights about what worked for them. While they were willing to talk about the various aspects of their strong and fulfilling relationships, and about the things they did to keep their marriages vibrant, they were, at the same time, quick to point out that their respective marriages were by no means perfect. (Unless otherwise indicated, we do not use people's real names, thus protecting their privacy.) We also drew upon the experience of our own marriage, the struggles, the satisfactions, the happiness. Together we reflected on the reasons for our sense of contentment and well-being.

Gradually, as we compiled what we heard and then reflected on our own personal experience, this book took shape. In the process we have distilled nine factors that seem essential in the nurturing of a successful marriage. There may be others, of course, but these nine proved to be prominent in marriages that had high levels of fulfillment and satisfaction.

Our intention is to offer this work as a support to busy married couples who do not have the time to read extensive volumes about relationships and family systems but who are open to trying a relatively simple approach to marital enrichment. We suggest that you read a chapter individually, individually respond to the questions at the end of that chapter ("Nurturing Dialogue"), and then share your responses. This technique generates the kind of dialogue that will, indeed, nurture your marriage and nudge it toward exciting growth and new possibilities.

We know that any marriage can be better, stronger, happier, healthier. We sincerely hope that in some small way this book will help bring about not just improvement but genuine enrichment for your marriage. By *doing* this *marriage work*, may your *marriage work better* than you ever imagined possible.

CHAPTER ONE

Little Things Mean a Lot

■ ■ ■ ■ ■

Bigger is not necessarily better when it comes to creating happy marriages. This is one significant thing we discovered in our conversations with dozens of married couples about what contributes to a lasting and satisfying marriage. Although dream homes, diamond rings, and expensive vacations may be memorable components in the life of a marriage, the little things are what actually cement a relationship into a lasting bond.

Consider what Alice and Don, happily married for thirty-seven years, told us about the turning point in their relationship:

Alice: I was always attracted to Don, but marriage is such a serious step that I wondered if he really was the right one. I could see that he possessed qualities I truly admired. He was kind, attentive, and had a great sense of humor, but for the longest time I just couldn't make up my mind about marrying him.

Don: I was beginning to get discouraged about my chances.

Alice: It was a box of chocolates that turned things around for us. Don and I both love chocolates, so when he won a box of expensive chocolates in a contest, we were ecstatic. Every day we each selected a chocolate to eat until finally there was just one piece left. It was one of Don's favorites, but you know what he did? He insisted that I eat it. I looked at him and started to cry. In an instant I knew that a man unselfish enough to give me the last chocolate was the man I wanted

7

to spend the rest of my life with. That night I agreed to marry him.

Don (laughing): And every year since then, on the anniversary of her acceptance of my proposal, there's been a box of those chocolates.

There are countless "little things" that can serve as the mortar that holds together the structure of a sound marriage.

Common courtesy: Small acts of kindness, understanding, and respect seem to go a long way in making a satisfying and successful marriage. Annie shares how her husband's courtesies have meant a great deal to her. "We have been happily married for sixty years—and Bill still holds open the car door for me. Whenever he does that, I feel so special, so cared for. He is the most courteous man I've ever known, and I am so proud to be his wife."

Healing words and loving silences: Many couples commented on the power of words and what they can do to and for a relationship. Words can heal or hurt, soothe or scald, build up or tear down, bring hope or create despair. "In a marriage, it is important that a husband and wife not lie to each other," says Tom, married to Marie for nearly fifty years. "Sometimes, though, words can be used like a club to bludgeon your partner—even if it's the truth. That is not to say you have to lie—but you don't always have to say what's on your mind, truthful though it may be."

Marie agrees. "I once heard that referred to as the 'ministry of holding your tongue.' Sometimes the greatest good is done by saying nothing at all."

Because the spoken word may well be remembered for years to come, happily married couples take care with what is and what is not said. They know the value of avoiding critical, nagging, and sarcastic language in favor of positive, encouraging, uplifting speech.

Compliments: Larry and Donna share their habit of complimenting each other at least once a day. "It's a habit we got into early in the marriage," says Donna. "In the evening, when I think about what happened during the day, I always stop and ask myself, *Now, how and when did I compliment Larry today?*

"Opportunities are everywhere, and so we just take advantage of them," adds Larry. "Today, for example, I complimented Donna on the way her hair looks."

"And I complimented him for the spirit of kindness I see in him and love so much," Donna chimes in.

Apologies and forgiveness: Loving couples emphasize the power of words, like "I'm sorry," "I apologize," "Please forgive me" to bring healing to the hurts that inevitably occur in marriage.

"My parents would never apologize to each other when something went wrong," shares Angela. "They could keep an argument alive and well sometimes for a week at a time. I made a vow to myself that I would never do that in my marriage. If I say or do something that is hurtful to my husband, I apologize to him right away, and he does the same to me. It's a way to stop things before they start getting out of hand, and it really does work."

Saying "I love you": When it comes to harnessing the power of words to build a better marriage, people who have enjoyed satisfying marriages agree that the most important words spouses can say to each other are "I love you."

Barbara: When Ben was overseas during the Vietnam War, he wrote me every day to tell me how much he loved me.

Ben: When I got home, I discovered it was something I wanted to continue doing. Now I not only tell her each day that I love her, but I often leave little notes around with that message on them—and she does the same for me. When I travel, I always find a love letter in my suitcase or briefcase. We try to say 'I love you' in as many ways as possible.

Thelma, widowed for eleven years, recalls those painful days when her husband, John, was dying. "We would hold hands and tell each other over and over, 'I love you. I love you.' And those were the last words he spoke to me. Even now, throughout the day, I will stop and say, 'John, I love you'—and sometimes I think I hear him answer just like he used to."

In a relationship as significant as marriage, spouses should not have to wonder about being loved. Yes, some people have a hard time actually saying, "I love you," but it's not impossible to utter these simple words. The very sound of "I love you" is important to the marital relationship; it needs to be said, preferably often.

When the "Little Things" Become Big Problems

Little things affect a marriage more than a couple may realize—for good and for ill. It's those little things that, day in and day out, can grow, carrying with them the power to erode an otherwise healthy relationship. In fact, little things have a way of looming large over time to the point where serious problems can result.

The little things—like continually finding the toilet seat left up, the cap left off the toothpaste, or clothes thrown helter-skelter—although seemingly insignificant, have a way of generating anger that may eventually result in a firestorm of a fight. Invariably, couples seem to realize that it's not so much the small incidents that matter, but the way they are interpreted.

Lori: Jim got into the habit of throwing a wet towel over the towel rack after his morning shower. Actually, he would sort of wad it up and cram it into the rack. I like the towels hanging straight, neat, and in place, especially in case company comes.

Jim: Generally, in the morning I'm in a hurry but still kinda tired, so I just don't pay much attention to what I am doing.

Lori: I reminded him about it over and over, but he continued to do the same thing. After awhile I started to feel hurt and angry. I actually convinced myself that he didn't care enough about my feelings to do something so extremely simple. I could feel my resentment growing.

Jim: Then our church sponsored an evening for married couples, including a time for dialogue. When Lori shared with me her feelings about this problem, it was as if a light bulb went on in my head. For the first time I saw how much it meant to Lori to have the towels hanging neatly. And since old habits die hard, I was afraid that I would cooperate with her for a while and then relapse. So I created a simple solution to our problem. I just put a hook behind the bathroom door where I can hang my towel to dry, leaving hers looking great. It was that easy.

Couples who repeatedly fight over small things need to ask themselves if the squabbling is really worth it. Endless bickering can eventually drain off the emotional energy from a marriage, leaving nothing for the really important things.

Sometimes, too, there may be hidden dynamics behind seemingly insignificant events. Little things, for example, can be reminders of huge hurts from the past. In fact, past events can strongly influence present ones.

Leanne and Tom, married ten years, have a solid marriage and are genuinely happy. They recall, however, how small incidents early in their marriage triggered strong reactions in Leanne.

Tom: When we were first married, I liked to watch television and have a beer in the living room. Sometimes I'd forget to pick up the can and dispose of it, though, and when Leanne saw the can, she'd get terribly upset, even break into tears. At first it didn't make any sense to me.

Leanne: My father was an alcoholic. He would come home, practically drink himself into a coma, and leave beer cans all over the living room. When I would bring my friends home, sometimes they would see the mess my dad made—they even saw him passed out on the floor one time. I was so embarrassed I wanted to die. Tom isn't messy, it's just seeing that one beer can! It brings back those painful memories.

Looking for the real meaning behind seemingly innocuous events and getting the right perspective can help married couples deal with small annoyances in more constructive, positive ways. Generally, this will be accomplished only if partners are willing to be honest, open, and vulnerable enough to disclose their deepest feelings about what is really going on inside of them.

Our Personal Experience

We have grown to appreciate the significant impact of little things in our own marriage. Here are five factors that, although small in themselves, have helped nurture our relationship.

1. Being attentive to one another: Being attentive means that we tune in to each other in considerate, caring ways, such as making eye contact when we talk. When we interact on the run, our interactions become impersonal, even dehumanizing. When we speak to each other, we make a conscious effort to pause in what we are doing to establish eye contact. This has become for us a sign of respect and it helps us feel more connected.

Being attentive also involves our recognition of each other's presence. We are attentive at the beginning of each day as we greet each other with "Good morning" and a kiss. We also acknowledge each other when we come home from work and with phone calls during the day, just to say hello and to see how things are going.

Attentiveness is a special way of focusing on each other. It says,

"You are important to me, important enough for me to give you my undivided attention. You are worth my time."

2. *Kindness:* Attentiveness leads to kindness. We have found that small acts of kindness greatly enrich our relationship—everything from bringing the other a cup of coffee in bed or a cold glass of lemonade while mowing the lawn, starting the other's car on a cold morning to let it warm up, or making a special late-night trip to the store to buy the other's favorite ice cream.

Agreeing to disagree kindly is a way of stopping anger before it gets started. Kindness gives birth to kindness. It brings forth the best from each of us.

3. *Touching:* Touch is one of the easiest and best ways for us to feel close. A kiss, a hug, a backrub, holding hands—these make us feel connected. As babies, we are touched all the time, but as we grow older touch usually becomes less frequent. Touch deprivation is something we avoid. We actually find that we cannot touch each other enough. We hold hands everywhere—in the car, at a theater, even in church. Touching generates a sense of togetherness and affection. We find touch to be good for us and good for our marriage.

4. *Gratitude:* We work hard to avoid taking each other for granted, a common tendency between spouses. We express our gratitude to each other every day, for the simplest of things. For us this means deliberately constructing an "attitude of gratitude." We make it a point to tell each other, "Thank you," "I appreciate what you did," "That meant a lot to me." We show our gratitude not only for things done but also for the fact that we exist, that we are together, that we are gifts to each other from God. In fact, our entire marital spirituality is based on thanksgiving.

5. *Praise:* We are sensitive to each other's need for praise and affirmation, when it's just the two of us and when we're in the presence of others. Affirmation comes from a Latin word meaning "to make

strong," and authentic praise is an excellent way for us to affirm each other, thus making our relationship stronger.

Praise is more than just being complimentary, however. It is a kind of validation that says to the other, "I value you so much that I want to underscore your finest qualities. I want to say them out loud, and I want others to know about them as well."

Through genuine praise, we find that the other's self-esteem is enhanced. It makes us aware of our special dignity and worth. It brings a dimension of healing to our marriage by helping us to believe in ourselves more, both as individuals and as spouses.

Marriage is a lifelong project that succeeds or fails largely on the basis of little things done or not done as the days unfold. Just as a home is built little by little, one piece at a time, so too with marriage; the little things, one thing at a time, collectively help create the structure of a marriage.

Nurturing Dialogue

1. What was the last little thing that my spouse did for me that I genuinely appreciated? Did I let my spouse know how much that little thing meant to me?
2. What was the last little thing that I did for my spouse that was similarly much appreciated? Was I thanked? How did I feel about being thanked or not being thanked?
3. When did I last tell my spouse "I love you"? Can I do that today?
4. What small things in our marriage could be potentially harmful to our relationship? How can the two of us best address and resolve those small things before they begin to weaken our relationship?

CHAPTER TWO

Making Love, Making Marriage

■ ■ ■ ■ ■

When the two of us envisioned this project, we decided to interview only two groups of people—those who were happily married and those who had been happily married while their spouses were alive. We made one exception to this process, however; we decided to include some observations from our pastor, a celibate Catholic priest, on the importance of a good sexual relationship in marriage.

Father Denis Spitzley, of the Diocese of Lansing, Michigan, has been a priest for over twenty-five years. He has prepared hundreds of couples for the sacrament of marriage and counsels married couples as they struggle with the complexities of intimate relating. Although he himself has never been married, Father Denis knows a great deal about marriage. According to Father Denis:

> Lovemaking in marriage has a special ability to heal hurts that may have accumulated throughout the day. A couple has a choice. They can go to bed angry, or they can make love and heal each other. The words "make love" say it all. Through physical intimacy a couple can make more love for their marriage. The first miracle of Jesus was at a wedding, where newlyweds had run out of wine. So, too, when a couple seems to be running out of love and affection for each other, they can make more love and more affection. What a gift! And that is why sexual pleasure in marriage is holy: it does what God does—it makes love.

Many of the couples we talked with seemed to reflect what Father Denis shared. Listen to what these couples of long and satisfying marriages have to share about lovemaking:

Elena: A good sexual relationship doesn't come with the marriage license, it's something that has to be worked on together and grown into together. You've both got to be patient and considerate of each other, and just keep practicing until you start getting it right.

Tom: Making love is more than having sex together. Good lovemaking flows out of a good friendship. That's why as your friendship grows, the sex only gets better and better.

Leo: We recently went on a train ride and the train broke down while we were passing through a long tunnel. We were told there would be a two-hour delay, so we made love right there in the coach.

Martha (laughing): You have to admit, it's a great way to pass the time.

Sam: Right from the beginning of our marriage we both have felt there is something spiritual about intercourse.

Terry: It's hard to put into words, and it goes beyond procreating our three children. It's a feeling of complete oneness with each other and with the whole universe.

Sam: Not all the time, but many times, making love has been almost a mystical experience. It's a kind of gateway to the soul—my soul and Terry's soul to the soul of God. We often say a prayer of thanksgiving afterward. It just seems the right thing to do after experiencing something so wonderful.

Sexuality and Creativity

Our society has a great fascination with anything sexual. Much of this fascination, however, is limited to the physical act itself—the frequency and intensity of orgasms, the latest discoveries about erogenous zones, and techniques guaranteed to ignite explosive sex.

We have no intention of downplaying the sheer physical pleasure that sex can bring. Spouses should freely enjoy that experience whenever possible and to the fullest extent possible. Marriage truly is the best and most appropriate place for full sexual expression, not just because of its procreative possibilities but because a sexual relationship belongs exclusively within the joys of a committed relationship.

Our own marital experience has taught us that we are growing together sexually just as we are growing together emotionally and spiritually. We are more sexually compatible at the present time, for example, than we were five years ago—and we expect to be even more compatible five years from now. We intend to keep our sexual relationship dynamic, ever-changing, exciting, and satisfying, and we take special care to guard our relationship against sexual complacency. We emphasize creativity.

The creation of a sound and satisfying sexual relationship in marriage requires time, effort, patience, great sensitivity, and loving creativity. Full sexual satisfaction is achieved not so much by mastering techniques for a grand sexual performance, as by creatively fostering unity and closeness outside the bedroom. Good sex comes from good love—and that takes creativity!

The Deeper Dimension of Sexuality

The pleasures and satisfactions of sex go far beyond physical pleasure, great as that is. Sex in marriage greatly enhances a couple's ability to communicate and understand each other. Words, after all, are only a small part of the communication process. Body language often says far more than words ever could, and sex is the ultimate body language.

The experience of physical intimacy gives new meaning to words like *love, tenderness, care,* and *reverence.* In fact, sex lends flesh to these words; they are no longer just words or concepts, but are felt physically, creating a whole new dimension of communication.

Sex is also a magnificent teacher, bringing great insight and knowledge that leads to growth, maturity, and deeper satisfaction. For example, in our sexuality we have consciously changed the emphasis from a preoccupation with having our personal needs met to focusing on satisfying the other's needs and desires—trying our best to make the other sexually happy and fulfilled. Simply learning to be attentive to each other and trying our best to please the other has enabled us to experience sexual fulfillment. In the giving comes the receiving, so that the whole sexual dimension of our lives is nurtured and enriched.

Sex also deepens love—which is exactly what a sexual relationship in marriage is supposed to do. Couples usually love each other before they experience physical intimacy. Then, when they sexually express themselves to each other in marriage, they feel the physical manifestation of the emotions and know themselves deeply loved—which then generates a mutually loving atmosphere that generates even greater love. Love creates love.

For us lovemaking has been a profound experience of love-expressing and love-sharing. It has brought a deep sense of solidarity to our marital relationship.

Sex deepens the loving friendship that spouses share. Creative and playful lovemaking intensifies the bond of friendship in which marriage takes its first roots. It has a way of smoothing out the rough edges, making the spouses more accepting of each other's faults. It is a total sharing in which friends discover that they can be lovers—and lovers discover that they can be friends.

Our Personal Experience

What follows is not advice but suggestions, drawn from our own marriage, that may prove helpful in nurturing and enriching your own sexual relationship.

1. *Protect your love life at all costs.* Your shared sexuality is one of the most important aspects of your marital relationship. Guard it from incursions by friends, social activities, work, and family, including children. You owe it to each other to make your sexual relationship a priority in your marriage. Yes, it is that big a deal.

2. *Make love often.* Lovemaking is the best way to stay close and connected. It reminds you, as nothing else can, that you are married to each other and that the two of you can still become one.

3. *Let your lovemaking mean more than intercourse.* There are many forms of sexual expression that bring pleasure and satisfaction. Being creative, even experimental, can infuse new excitement in your relationship. Variety is, indeed, the spice of life, and that includes your sex life. Because this is a highly sensitive area, be especially sensitive with each other. Rely on your mutual trust and be in full agreement as you explore new approaches.

4. *Talk to each other about your sex life.* Many couples who have no difficulty engaging in sex have major problems talking about it with each other. Yet this is one area where communication is imperative. Keep your sexual relationship satisfying by talking about your likes and dislikes, your pleasures and preferences, your satisfactions and disappointments. Is there room for improvement in your sexual relationship? If so, can you agree on what needs to change? Is lovemaking frequent enough for both of you? Good communication can lead to not just *good* sex, but *great* sex, especially if you are both willing to be open, accepting, and nonjudgmental.

5. Stay affectionate through touching. Don't let sex become your primary form of touching. In fact, touch each other as much as you can: hug, kiss, caress, give backrubs and massages, hold hands, walk with your arms around each other. Touching keeps you physically connected and can help you feel valued and loved. Touch does not have to lead to sex. In fact, simple touch can generate a deeply sensual experience in which you are aware of how wonderful it feels to have a body. By gaining an appreciation for the pleasures of the senses, nonsexual touching can help you enjoy your sexual experiences even more.

6. *Make romance a part of your sexual relationship.* It isn't difficult to create a romantic environment that will help keep desire alive and fuel passion. Flowers, candlelight, dancing, making love in front of a crackling fire—these are the kinds of things that can change the familiar act of having sex into a truly intimate experience of making love. If you have children, you may need to be deliberate and conscientious about arranging your romantic interludes. Don't hesitate to treat yourself to a child-free evening or weekend by securing a reliable person to provide childcare in your absence. Your relationship is worth it.

Fostering romance need not involve a major financial investment. Being romantic involves recognizing opportunities and availing yourself of them to spice up your marital relationship.

7. *Bring something new and different to your love life.* Like all things human, sex can become routine and humdrum if it is always done in the same way, at the same time, and in the same place. Providing the two of you are open and flexible, perhaps it's time for some changes. Christian bookstores carry books that offer suggestions about different sexual techniques and options. Since many of us are still woefully ignorant about the dynamics of human sexuality, especially male-female differences, acquiring more information and knowledge about your bodies can be beneficial to your sexual relationship.

8. Remember that sex is a mirror of your marriage. We become better lovers as we become better spouses. That is why marriage enrichment programs, retreats for couples, Marriage Encounter weekends, or marital skill-building classes are so popular and readily available. They can teach couples how to communicate and strengthen their bond.

9. Be aware of the factors that affect your love life, both positively and negatively. Alcohol, for example, may increase sexual desire, but it diminishes performance, and heavy smoking can halt sex altogether. High levels of stress, emotional tensions, burnout, and exhaustion can virtually eliminate any desire for lovemaking. Building anger management skills may help remove barriers to satisfying sex. Reducing stress whenever possible not only keeps us more relaxed but actually improves overall health, and good health is important to good sex. Regular exercise can have the effect of an aphrodisiac; it gives us more energy and stamina.

10. Get help if you need it. Research in the field of human sexuality is providing better understanding with regard to sexual satisfaction. For example, until recently sexual dysfunction was largely attributed to psychological causes. We now know, however, that most sexual dysfunction is due to physical conditions. A competent physician trained in gynecology or urology can correct many of these physical problems. New medications are practically eliminating certain sexual problems that were once considered untreatable.

Not all sexual problems, however, are physical. People who have been victims of damaging abusive behavior, particularly sexual abuse, can carry lasting scars. If you have struggled with this issue, now may be the time to begin the quest for healing. It could change your life and your marriage forever.

A number of the couples we talked to told us that, like good wine, their love life was getting better with age. As the years go by, may we all age gracefully as friends and lovers.

Nurturing Dialogue

1. How has our sexual relationship changed from the beginning of our marriage to the present? Are the changes good? If not, why not?

2. What do I enjoy most about our lovemaking? What don't I like about our lovemaking?

3. Is there something different or new I would like to try?

4. Do I see any obstacles in our love life that prevent either or both of us from experiencing deep sexual satisfaction? If so, what are they? What might we do about them? Are we comfortable enough with each other to talk about our options?

5. What might we do together to enrich our lovemaking? How might I take better care of myself physically and emotionally so that I bring a healthier me to lovemaking with my spouse?

CHAPTER THREE

Making Your Marriage a Holy Trinity: Husband, Wife, and God

■ ■ ■ ■ ■

Researchers who study marriages point out that a spiritual dimension increases both the happiness and the stability of the marital relationship. That is exactly what we found when we asked couples about how and where God fits into their married life. Many responded with surprising candor, even a sense of gratitude for being asked about the spiritual component of their relationship. For many couples this was the first time anyone had asked them about God's place in their marriage, the first time they were provided an opportunity to talk about their spiritual experience in marriage. Here is some of what we heard.

Paul: We decided early in our marriage that we would make the choice to let Christ into our married life. It was the best decision we ever made.

Elaine: The Lord has been a kind of invisible force holding us together during the times when we couldn't do it by ourselves. And as we've drawn closer to him, we've also drawn closer to each other. We couldn't imagine a marriage without his presence.

■

Sharon (a widow): Roy and I felt from the very beginning of our relationship, even before we married, that God had brought us together, so a God-centered marriage was what we wanted, and with God's help, it was something we achieved. We did this mostly by learning to pray together. I don't mean just saying prayers together. We really prayed from our hearts. Every day Roy and I would hold hands and talk to God about our lives. After all those years of praying, our spirits seemed to merge into one.

Linda: My parents were devout Christians. They never missed church, said grace before every meal, and at the end of the day, they knelt down together for night prayers. But I have no recollection of them ever discussing their faith or sharing their experiences of God with each other. Maybe they did privately, I don't know. I just knew that when I married, I wanted to share everything with my husband, especially my faith walk and my faith stories.

Larry: We make it a point to regularly talk to each other about how we see God working in our lives, and how we can better serve God. When you view your marriage through the eyes of faith, it changes your perspective. You tend to ask, *Now, what would God want us to do in this situation?* That outlook has helped us build a strong spiritual life together and has really blessed our marriage.

A number of couples told us how they reached the point in their marriage where simply being good company for each other was no longer enough. They grew dissatisfied with a common garden-variety type of marriage and wanted more. Harnessing the energy of their spirits provided that for many of them.

Our Personal Experience

Spiritual growth is a lifelong process, and we learn more about it every day. We have used the following tools to spiritually energize our marriage. May they benefit you as well.

1. Prioritize the gift of time to nurture your spiritual life. Like many married couples, our lives are busy with juggling careers and the needs of family. However, we do not let our busy schedules keep us from consciously and deliberately taking and making time for things like prayer, Scripture study, and worship—together.

The spiritual side of marriage will not simply develop on its own without effort. It has to be nurtured, and this requires the investment of time. We find that the more time we set aside for spiritual opportunities, the more our marriage is enriched and blessed—and if we fail to do this, we feel the impact of that choice almost immediately. We begin to sense that some life-giving part of our relationship is not thriving. If we are too busy to nurture the spirituality of our marriage, we are too busy—*period!*

2. Deal with anger before it torpedoes your spiritual journey together. It is difficult to pray with your spouse or, for that matter, to pursue anything spiritual together, if you are angry. Unresolved anger can destroy a marriage from the inside like dry rot. It prevents spiritual growth—or any other kind of growth—from taking place.

You cannot live together, of course, without getting angry with each other; that is normal. It's the persistent state of anger that will damage a marriage.

Consider asking yourselves some basic questions, such as: *Is this really worth getting angry over? Will this issue matter a week from now?* Most of the time, you will find that the answer is "no," and you are able to release the anger and free yourselves emotionally for truly important things.

There is an old saying: "Anger pushes love out of the heart."

The danger to the spiritual part of a marriage is that anger can push God out as well. Anger needs to be carefully monitored and controlled before it begins to negatively affect the marriage.

3. Create or seek out an environment where your spirit is at home. It may be in a church, a retreat house, a meadow or forest, or a room in your home set aside for quiet meditation.

We increasingly experience God's presence together in nature. Medical researchers describe natural settings as "restorative environments." They have rediscovered an ancient truth modern society has forgotten, that the beauty of nature can help heal the injured body, mind, and spirit.

Just being together in a natural environment gives us a sense of God's goodness and provides us an opportunity for communion with God and each other. The right environment sets the stage for the spiritual—and for quality time at its very best.

4. Sacrifice for the good of your marriage. The word *sacrifice* comes from two Latin words that mean "to make holy." When we engage in genuine "sacrificial activity," we do, in fact, bring a holy dimension to our marriage.

Sacrifice means different things to different people, of course. It can mean giving something up for a greater good, for example, like giving up the urge to retaliate or get even after we feel we've been wronged or hurt. It can mean giving up the desire to have things our own way in favor of understanding our spouse's point of view. It can mean letting go of the need to "be right" or "to win" every argument. It can mean saying "no" to a social invitation that would take us away from home and, instead, spending time with our spouse building up our marriage.

Sacrifice can mean caring for our spouse to the point where it hurts—doing far more than might be expected, going the extra mile. It is a way of loving extravagantly, generously, lavishly.

Sacrificial activity is uniquely Christlike. It was Jesus, after all, who said that great love is willing to prove itself by laying down one's life for one's friends (see John 15:13). Jesus then went on to provide us with the supreme example of sacrificial love.

Bringing this kind of love to your marriage is no easy task but when it is achieved, it has the power to transform your marriage, precisely because it is so God-like.

5. Make service a part of your marriage. Service is closely connected to sacrifice. Jesus said that he came not to *be served*, but to *serve* (see Matthew 20:28). We simply cannot walk with him, at least not very far, before he asks us to begin serving in his name.

Unfortunately, the difficulty with our contemporary model of marriage is that it is based almost entirely on the notion of self-fulfillment. Many of us enter marriage believing—consciously or unconsciously—that our partner exists to meet our needs. When that does not happen—and it will, in fact, not happen—disillusionment sets in and, not infrequently, the relationship crashes and burns. We then go on to a new relationship with the same set of expectations.

The Gospels, however, give us a different model, one that is relevant to marriage today: we have been saved by God to serve. Thus, an important ingredient of Christian marriage is service, and our first responsibility is to serve our spouse, to put the best interests of our spouse above our own. From there, the Lord directs us to bring this same serving love to our family and friends, and then, in a broader sense, to the entire world.

In our marriage, for example, we strive to serve God with our financial resources. Part of our tithe goes to those organizations that are instrumental in feeding the poor and taking care of the homeless and needy. We believe that in this way, we are serving humanity and pleasing God as a married couple.

Bringing a service mentality to marriage is truly countercultural. It flies in the face of what our society has to say about marriage. Yet, in viewing our marriage as a form of "servanthood," serving each other, our family, and our world in the name of Jesus Christ, we have found a special kind of joy and fulfillment—a joy and fulfillment that can be understood only by doing it.

6. *Daily recommit yourselves to each other.* Scripture speaks of God's absolute commitment to us, and much of the time the image of marriage is used to describe that commitment.

Commitment in marriage means that I have bonded my life to yours in the past, that I choose to respect and nurture that bond today, in the present, and that I will continue to make that same choice tomorrow and every day of our lives, until death parts us. I choose to walk down the path of life with you, and will never abandon or forsake you or our bond.

We believe that commitment means so much more than just living together, sharing the same house and bed, and managing the same household budget and chores. In the fullest sense, commitment is the willingness to grow together, to move forward into the future together, and to do whatever we can to foster our unity and closeness. We recommit to each other on a daily basis. We affirm that our relationship takes precedence over all other relationships, even those with our children.

A friend of ours recently told us of her experience of breast cancer and the accompanying double mastectomy. Before surgery, she worried about how this might affect her relationship with her husband. When she shared her anxiety with him, however, he told her that he loved her for who she was, who she is, and who she is yet to be—and nothing would change that. This is marital commitment.

Commitment creates stability in the marital relationship. It provides a solid foundation upon which all growth, especially spiritual growth, can take place. Without commitment, the meaning of the past, the reality of the present, and the hope of the future are at the mercy of the changing times.

7. *Listen to each other.* There is a strong link between listening to each other and developing a deeper relationship with God. Listening to God is the essence of prayer. Only by learning to listen to

God, in the many and varied ways God speaks to us, are we able to discover what God wants from us and for us—that is, God's will for our lives. By listening we come to know who God is, what God is really like.

So, too, genuine listening enables us to truly know and understand our spouse. A famous theologian wrote that the first duty of love is to listen. Listening fosters the growth of love and leads to deeper intimacy, the state of being close. In our marriage, listening helps us draw closer to each other and to God. It is an invaluable tool that helps us create and maintain a marital spirituality.

A lasting and satisfying marriage is actually a holy trinity—husband, wife, and God. Because God never comes into our lives by force, God comes into a marriage only by invitation. We need to ask God in. Only with that Third Partner will the spiritual dimension of marriage be real and abiding. As finite human beings, we cannot meet all of each other's needs, bring each other total happiness, or ensure complete and lasting fulfillment. Only God can do these things. Only God's grace can give us the insight and understanding—about our self, our partner, and our commitment to each other—we need to enjoy the lasting fruits of marriage.

Nurturing Dialogue

1. When have I been very much aware of God's presence in my life, when have I felt particularly close to God? Could I share this experience with my spouse?
2. How would I describe the spiritual dimension of our marriage?
3. How do I see our marriage growing spiritually? What might we do to enhance spiritual growth in our marriage?
4. Are there any barriers to spiritual growth in our marriage? If so, what are they? How might we work together as a couple and with God's grace to remove them?
5. Which of the seven tools to spiritually energize marriage are the most appealing to me personally? How might I use those specific tools in our marriage?

CHAPTER FOUR

The Time of Our Lives: Time Together and Time Apart

■ ■ ■ ■ ■

As we dialogued with people about marriage and their own personal experience of marriage, we found that many couples had worked out their own systems of marital time management. In their own way, they achieved a healthy balance between the time they spent together and the time they spent apart.

Time apart was particularly noteworthy because the majority did not use those opportunities as "escapes," but as times to renew themselves in ways that permitted them to return to their partners as healthier and better integrated individuals. This, in turn, affected the marriage in positive ways.

Lillian's story is typical of others we heard. She was happily married for twenty years when her husband, Al, was killed in an automobile accident. She describes their struggle to achieve a balance between time together and time apart.

"When Al and I were first married, we nearly suffocated each other with too much togetherness. The only time we were apart was when we went to work and when we went to the bathroom. Otherwise, we did everything together.

"Now, I dearly loved Al, but after a while, I began to feel that something was missing from our marriage. I thought about it for a long time before I realized what it was: Neither of us had any personal space and time in which to refill our cups—and this was beginning to take quite a toll on our relationship. One day I finally sat Al down and told him that I wanted him to go back to playing poker on Friday nights with his old buddies, and that I was joining a bowling league.

"He was delighted! He had wanted to play poker with his friends but thought I might feel abandoned or hurt if he did."

Did this help the marriage?

"You bet it did! It began to take some pressure off us to be everything to each other all the time. As the years went by, Al and I looked for opportunities to do things together, but we also did many things apart. We even established friendships outside the marriage. All this was good for us and helped us appreciate each other even more. When I think about those times, I find myself saying thank you to God—for poker and bowling. They very possibly saved our marriage."

Intimacy is nurtured by quality time—time spent together, when a couple is fully attentive to each other and strive to create a feeling of closeness, and time spent apart, when the individual spouses explore their own interests in ways that allow their unique gifts to flourish. Healthy intimacy recognizes that the individual must be allowed to nurture his or her unique personhood as long as it does not weaken the marriage. The challenge, of course, is to be flexible and confident enough about the relationship so as not to be threatened when the other starts to grow and develop in new and different ways.

Quality Time Together

As you consider how you might spend quality time together as a couple, keep in mind that what, when, and how you spend time together is uniquely yours to decide. There is no set of criteria other than that you are enjoying each other in the activity. The following list of guidelines might help you explore and make decisions about your quality time together.

Date each other again. Think back to the time before you married; remember the fun, the excitement? Remember how you looked forward to your "dates"? Begin dating again. Pick a night that works for your schedule, and make that your special night together—either away from home or even without leaving your home. For example, you can share a movie at a theater or simply rent a video and hold hands watching on the couch. Sit down together each month and determine which nights will be your "date nights," circle them on a calendar, and don't let anything interfere with your plans. This is your time together. Enjoy.

Go for a walk together. We all admire couples who walk together holding hands; there is something warm and intimate about a couple holding hands. You can do the same thing. A power walk done at a brisk pace hardly lends itself to hand-holding, but a more leisurely stroll will. Walk together and talk together. It may well be the highlight of your day.

Take a class together. The opportunity to learn new things together can be an especially intimate experience. As your minds explore new ideas, new concepts, you find yourselves talking about things you may never have considered worth your time and effort. A cooking class, art class, or literature class can offer you lasting benefits for years to come. One caveat: don't be competitive or turn this venture into an ego trip. No grandstanding allowed. The idea is not to find out who is the smartest or who has the most talent; the "grade" is hardly important. This will only work if a couple truly is interested in growing together.

Dance together as often as you can. The old song lyric that says "you're in heaven when you are dancing" may not be far from the truth. Style and class are not important; being together is. No one will be judging your performance, and it will make you feel good about yourselves and your marriage.

Cuddle. Many of the widows and widowers we talked to said that they miss cuddling the most—cuddling in bed at the end of the day, cuddling on the couch, cuddling on the porch swing. "On stormy nights," remembers Anne, "my husband and I would go to bed early and just hold each other and talk about everything under the sun. I always felt so safe and snug. I never wanted those evenings to end."

Develop common interests you both enjoy. Cook a meal together, garden together, play golf together, or go fishing together. Common interests not only help a couple stay close, they also offer a means of relaxation. Fun activities help drain away the stress and worries from our lives and enable us to reconnect to our spouse. A couple we admire play musical instruments together—she plays the piano and he accompanies her on the violin. Anyone watching them play can tell they have achieved a happy and fulfilling relationship. At times it seems as though they can read each other's minds. In the fullest sense they have learned to make beautiful music together, even when they are not playing their instruments. Certain sports also allow a couple to function as a team, and the experience of teamwork is good.

Vacation together. A vacation refreshes individuals and marriages. Make it as elaborate or simple as you like, as you can comfortably afford. Some couples stay home, others go away. We thought that Jim and Louise, married fifteen years, had a great idea with their monthly vacation concept. "We take twelve vacations a year," Jim told us, "one each month. A vacation for us means that we get away from home together for at least an overnight. During the cold months we go to a hotel with a pool. During the nice weather we camp. Once a year we make a retreat together. We budget the money for these vacations much the same way we budget for other important items. We have some wonderful experiences, thanks to these vacations."

Touch at every opportunity. The most ordinary times can be transformed into quality times just by touching. Holding hands at the mall, in the car, or at a restaurant, hugging and kissing before work and at the end of the work day, giving each other a back rub while watching television—in a word, touching can make a huge difference in the ways we experience and perceive things.

The best things in a marriage are not necessarily the big things. Seemingly insignificant events can become truly memorable if we adopt a mindset that looks for ways to create quality time.

Achieving Quality Time Apart

Quality time *apart* is just as important as quality time *together*. Without your private time, time for your own personal interests and pleasures, quality time together ultimately will lack something critical—the two of you as well-integrated individuals. The following suggestions serve as guidelines for developing your own independent quality time apart.

Explore your own gifts and talents. Perhaps you're not even sure what your gifts and talents are. With quality time for yourselves, you have the opportunity to go on a self-adventure that can unearth a wealth of personal treasures. Your gifts and talents have been given to each of you for a purpose you may not discover unless you let them emerge and bloom.

Many persons attest to the fact that some of the finest moments of their lives have taken place when they gave free reign to their own unique gifts and as a consequence, experienced deep joy and self-fulfillment. Being married is by no means a barrier to this kind of exploration into your individual identities.

Develop your own friendships and spend time with your friends. Friendships outside marriage can be highly beneficial for your relationship. Having other friends takes pressure off of each of you, individually and as a couple. The truth is there are some things we share with our friends that, for a variety of reasons, we may choose not to share with our spouse. There are activities we do with our friends that may not be of interest to our spouse.

Having other good friends along with our marriage partner makes us feel less alone. Friendships can also provide a valuable support system that brings happiness and stability to our lives and thus to the marriage.

Take responsibility for your own happiness. Couples can get into trouble when one spouse expects the other to make him or her completely happy. As the old saying goes, happiness is an inside job. By investing time in ourselves, especially by coming to greater self-knowledge through which we become aware of what our deepest needs really are, we can open doors to greater happiness. Listen to your heart. Follow where your dreams lead you. Pursue your own happiness.

Pamper yourself. On occasion it is good to be unusually kind to ourselves as individuals. Treating yourself to a massage, sleeping in late, buying yourself that mega-calorie ice cream, or getting that special golf club you've always wanted can be ways of rewarding yourself and helping you enjoy life more. Go ahead—spoil yourself. Finding pleasure just for ourselves should have a place in every marriage

Meditate. Meditation is a uniquely individual experience that does many things for the mind, body, and soul. It reduces stress and allows you to relax; it allows you to get in touch with your body; it taps into your spiritual life and opens spaces of quiet where the presence of God can be realized. Meditation can be a powerful means for self-discovery and personal growth, thus representing quality time at its very best.

Be yourself and cherish that self. If you define yourself solely in terms of your marriage, you risk losing a true sense of who you are. After all, you had an identity long before you were married. Be yourself, who you really are. The connection between being yourself and experiencing quality time is basic. The more genuine you are, the better choices you will make with regard to your own good, and the better choices you make for yourself, the better choices you will make with your spouse for your relationship.

Keep learning and growing. Marriage is not meant to be the end of the line when it comes to personal growth and development. Investing your time in the pursuit of new skills and other forms of learning is a way to stay energized and flexible, ready to adapt to the inevitability of change. Working on your own growth keeps you young-thinking and open to new possibilities. Learning and growing brings zest to you and to your marriage.

Make healthy choices and invest some of your time in making them happen. For example, consider choosing to exercise, even in the light of other demands. Losing weight, giving up smoking, working on your fears and self-limiting behaviors, becoming more assertive, forgiving yourself for real or imagined mistakes and failings, joining a recovery program that helps you deal with chemical dependency or pain from childhood, learning to control your emotions, taking control of your personal finances—choices such as these can give you a sense of personal respect and power. You discover that you can make positive, healthy changes in your life, and that they, in turn, can have a positive, healthy impact on your marriage.

Our Personal Experience

Although finding ways to enjoy quality time together and quality time apart can be challenging, we find it rewarding to ourselves as individuals and to our marriage. For example, together, we prioritize our prayer time. We look forward to our morning ritual, during which we hold hands, pray together, and share a lingering kiss. Even though the actual prayer often is brief, we savor those moments. That time together makes us feel close to God and to each other—not a bad way to begin the day.

We also enjoy reminiscing together. We like to share our childhood stories and remember together the time we first met and began to fall in love. We frequently share memories that pop into our minds at unexpected moments, finding this a way of sharing a part of ourselves that we may have otherwise overlooked—something the other would not know if we didn't capture the moment to share the memory. And since not all memories are good, the sharing sometimes becomes an act of trust that we will be accepted unconditionally, no matter what.

Many couples keep scrapbooks, photo albums, and home movies as a way to chronicle their individual and family history. Such "archives" generate the family stories that help people keep in touch with their roots from one generation to the next. Reminiscing gives a couple a sense of continuity and shared history and highlights their accomplishments together.

We also enjoy our individual time, not as times of "escape" or "relief," but as special gifts that allow us to explore more of our personal selves. In fact, like most couples, we have no desire whatsoever to spend one hundred percent of our time with each other. We need time for ourselves, and there is nothing wrong with that. We are conscientious about encouraging each other to take that time—without guilt or pressure—to do some self-exploration, self-nurturing, self-caring. We recognize and acknowledge this as a basic need that warrants being fulfilled at certain times. We give ourselves and each other permission to do what we need to do with and for ourselves.

One way we do this is by maintaining interests outside the marriage. The world is bigger than our marriages so, naturally, we are attracted to interests that go beyond the relationship. These interests prevent stagnation and boredom from creeping into our lives and become a source of tremendous enrichment. Our basic premise is that what's good for us as individuals is good for us as a couple.

It would seem that most couples go through periods of being close and being distant. At times, the need for intimacy will be paramount, only to be offset by the need for separate pursuits. All of this is normal and is, in fact, beneficial to the marriage.

For each of us time is a limited gift. Learning how to spend it wisely and well to meet our own personal needs as well as the needs arising from the very special and demanding relationship called marriage will be a lifelong challenge.

Nurturing Dialogue

1. Do we spend enough quality time together? If not, what could we do to increase quality time together?
2. If I should need more space and time to fulfill some of my own needs, would my spouse find that acceptable or threatening? Could I talk with my spouse about this important need?
3. Is there something that one of us has always wanted to do that we could do together? How could we go about doing it?
4. Is there something I would like to pursue that would enhance my own personal growth and perhaps make me feel better personally? Is there something my spouse would like to pursue that would enhance personal growth and perhaps make my spouse feel better personally? How could we help each other achieve these goals?
5. If I knew I had only one day left to spend with my spouse, how would I like to spend our time together?

CHAPTER FIVE

Creating by Relating: Staying Connected by Talking to Each Other

■ ■ ■ ■ ■

A lmost one hundred percent of the couples we interviewed felt that the most important marital skill is good verbal communication—the ability to talk to your partner about anything and everything, and have the feeling that you are being listened to with focused attention.

Here is a sampling of the wisdom we heard:

"You have to learn to accept and understand each other, and the only way that will happen is by talking *to* each other— not *at* each other."

"A husband and wife should be able to talk to each other about everything—good, bad, and indifferent. When you talk you settle things, and you can also prevent some bad things from happening."

"When you're mad at each other, get things out in the open as fast as you can before they start to fester. Yell and holler if you must, but keep on talking until you get things settled. That's the way to stay married."

"When spouses don't talk to each other, they begin to feel like they don't matter, like they're not important. Talking together helps you share information, ideas, dreams, and fears. It's the only way to really be *in* a relationship."

In general, good communication is one of the most satisfying of all human experiences; some say that good communication is even more satisfying than sex. We suggest that *sex itself* is an important form of communication.

Good communication is accomplished by more than just words, of course; factors such as body language, tone of voice, and eye contact are important to honest and complete communication. But verbal communication remains the bedrock; it is crucial to the life of a marriage. Lorraine and Dan share their struggles with good verbal communications:

Lorraine: My father was like Gary Cooper—the strong, silent type. When I married Dan, I soon realized that he was just like my dad; he didn't talk either. But the more I tried to force Dan to talk, the more he seemed to pull away, until finally we were barely saying anything at all to each other. Then we really were in trouble.

Dan: It was not that I didn't want to talk to Lorraine; I just didn't know how to do it. In my family we spoke only when it was necessary, and we talked only about things—certainly not about our feelings. The more she pushed, the more helpless I felt—and the more resentment grew in both of us. It was definitely a no-win situation.

Lorraine and Dan found themselves in a painful situation. Although we can understand why their marital communication patterns were difficult, we can also see that they were at risk of serious problems. What turned things around for them?

Lorraine: Marriage counseling. After years of near silence, we knew it was time to get help, because our marriage was starting to unravel. The therapist helped us recognize that the behaviors we brought to the marriage didn't work right from the beginning and certainly weren't working now. She also helped me deal with my obsessive need to change Dan.

Dan: And she showed me some simple communication skills that I began to practice at home.

Lorraine: About six months after we started counseling, we were talking to each other more than we ever had before. After eight months, we couldn't shut up.

Dan: There was so much I wanted to say to Lorraine that I never felt safe saying before. It was wonderful. The counseling was a serious investment of time and money, but it was well worth it. It taught us how to talk to each other.

Talking and Listening

Talking and listening help fuel a marriage in the same way gasoline fuels a vehicle; without it, no progress is possible. Talking and listening *gets a marriage going and keeps it going.* When a couple stops talking and listening to each other for whatever reasons—anger, fatigue, moodiness—there is an immediate sense of distancing, and they begin to feel out of alignment with each other. When they resume dialogue, they feel reconnected.

Talking and listening are obviously two sides of the same coin, the coin being good communication. If we are not clear, honest, and respectful in what we want to say and how we say it, we cannot expect attentive and empathic listening. Likewise, if we do not listen with our full attention and heart, we cannot expect our partner to put much effort into what he or she says. Why are talking and listening so vital to nurturing a marriage?

Talking and listening help you validate each other and foster respect. When one of you is talking and the other is listening and you know you are connecting, something good happens to your sense of self-worth—as individuals and as a couple. You naturally feel affirmed by your partner—an affirmation that goes beyond simple courtesy to full respectful validation.

Talking and listening help create intimacy. There are different levels of talking and listening, of course. Sharing the facts and details of your day-to-day lives goes a long way in keeping harmony within marriage. For example, not telling your spouse that you will be late for dinner not only ruins the evening, but it's just plain discourteous. Your partnership relies on sharing basic information.

But there is a deeper kind of talking and listening that helps stabilize your relationship in the richness of intimacy. This kind of talking and listening is based on self-disclosure, the kind of sharing that comes from deep within the heart.

Intimacy, the state of being close, cannot and will not come into existence merely by living together and sharing basic information on a day-to-day basis. Rather, intimacy is created and nurtured as you talk to your partner about who you are, what you really think and feel, what your most meaningful life experiences are, where you find your greatest joys and fears.

Authentic, honest talking and listening allow the human masks to be removed, so that the inner person is revealed. You come to know your partner—and yourself—only through the intimacy of healthy talking and listening. This is where you come to know the experience of being soul mates, where you realize the profound feeling of being fully known and accepted by another human being—and this closeness is the essence of marriage.

Talking and listening strengthen the bond of friendship. Friendship in marriage is characterized by an ability to talk about anything, knowing that you will not be put down or judged by your partner for what you say. Friendship in marriage creates an atmosphere of freedom in which talking flows easily and listening is a joy. By talking and listening to each other, you learn how to make your marital friendship stronger and more dynamic.

Talking and listening help resolve conflicts. Sooner or later, all couples face some form of conflict. Talking and listening are the only effective tools for working through those times of conflict with confidence. The way you face today's conflict will set your expectations for how you handle tomorrow's conflict.

Conflict resolution usually involves naming the problem and looking at all options. The dynamic of talking and listening allows both of you the opportunity to participate in this process. After all, seldom does one person know exactly *what the problem is* and *what solutions are best.* Rather, talking and listening brings all "sides" of the conflict into focus so that effective problem solving can be pursued.

Talking and listening make you feel more married—because you are *more married.* Before we got married, we both lived alone for many years. Now, as a married couple, we thoroughly enjoy the luxury of having a partner with whom we can engage in the simple joy of talking and listening. As we talk to each other, we are reminded that we are, indeed, married, that we share our lives in deep and intimate ways, and that we are vital in each other's life. For us, talking and listening have become almost like making love. There is so much giving of ourselves and receiving of the other.

The Skills that Deepen Good Communication

Good communication in marriage—talking and listening to each other—is a skill. As Lorraine and Dan shared earlier, we do not marry automatically knowing how to engage in good communication that will nurture a lifelong relationship. Good communication is a skill that often needs to be learned.

The following suggestions can help you begin to set a course for developing good communication skills. In addition to these suggestions, we strongly encourage you to seek out other resources on good communicating.

Keep your expectations realistic. There is no such thing as perfect communication in marriage. Sure, a couple might feel like they're right on the mark most of the time—talking clearly and constructively and being listened to with attention and empathy. At times, however, partners can be left feeling frustrated, like they did not express themselves clearly or did not understand something important. They feel like they're just not on the same wavelength—like they're each from some different, distant planet.

The solution? Don't give up; too much is at stake. Remind yourselves that you are not communication experts. Remind yourselves that good communication comes with practice, practice, practice. Above all, remind yourselves that you love each other. Don't let your poor communication deteriorate into a battle of wits or a fierce game of "oneupmanship." This is your marriage. Just keep talking!

Don't compare yourself to other married couples. What seems to work for one couple may not work for you. Remember, too, that what you hear and see is not always the genuine dynamic that a couple uses in the privacy of their own lives when a pressing issue is causing conflict. Create your own communication style tailored for your unique needs. And by all means, "If it ain't broken, don't fix it!" Improve upon it, yes, but don't dismantle it, unless you are sure that its replacement will work better.

Find a place where you talk and listen. Once again, this will be different from couple to couple, and will depend, to a great extent, on your preferences. Some couples do their best talking and listening over that first cup of coffee at the kitchen table in the morning. Others find they can be their best selves and can listen most attentively in the dark quiet of their bedroom at the end of the day. For us it's the couch in our family room. There we feel physically relaxed and secure with each other. Sitting on the couch, side by side, in close proximity to each other, we feel inclined to talk.

Your special place should be free from distractions and interruptions, a place where you can give each other your undivided attention. Once you identify your special talking-and-listening place, use it together as often as you can.

Establish a good time for talking and listening. Every life has a certain rhythm to it. This is true too for the life of a marriage. With time, your relationship develops a certain rhythm that comes from your daily routine. Get in touch with the rhythm of your relationship, and determine those times when you can be most present to each other—then make that time your own. Just as you allot time to do other important things together—such as going to church, shopping, and recreating—you have to allot your talking-and-listening time. It might be Tuesday night after supper, over breakfast at a restaurant on Saturday morning, or during a leisurely Sunday afternoon walk. We know several couples who regularly get a baby-sitter so that they are able to get away from home—from the all interruptions and distractions—just so they can talk and listen to and with each other.

Married couples often lament the fact that their lives are so busy that they feel like two ships passing in the night. After awhile they realize that there is hardly any depth to their communication. Scheduling time together for the sole purpose of talking and listening enables you keep in touch with each other—the bedrock of a satisfying marriage.

Make good use of body language. Good communication—talking and listening—starts with what you say and what you hear. Beyond that, your body plays a critical role. Something as simple as frequent and steady eye contact can make a considerable difference in the quality of what you say and what you hear. Often conversations between spouses are squeezed in on the run, sometimes with barely a glance at each other. They may convey information, but they are not likely to convey much affection.

Looking into the eyes of your spouse creates a certain intimate atmosphere. It helps say: "You have my full attention. I am listening to you and care about what you have to say. I want to be close to you. I am not thinking about what happened today or what I'm going to do tomorrow. I am listening to you because I'm interested in what you are saying."

Touching is another form of body language that enhances talking and listening. A light touch on the hand, for example, conveys a caring presence that enhances both talking and listening. While it conveys care, it also generates a sense of oneness, a sense that the two of you are sharing the same life and are very focused about that life in the present moment.

Our Personal Experience

We find that being spontaneous, creative, and playful helps us build good communications in our marriage. To us, talking to each other is not a duty; it's a delight—a critical delight. We even enjoy talking and listening to each other about fun and creative ways we might explore for the very purpose of improving our communication. We know of some couples who use their pool or jacuzzi as a place where they can playfully talk and listen to each other. Some couples find camping, sleeping out under the stars or in a tent, to be a wonderful opportunity for memorable conversations. Changing the setting simply adds something different—a certain spice—that can help communication become more meaningful and intimate.

We know, of course, that talking and listening to each other is the work—and play—of a lifetime. We remain alert to those opportunities that might help us enhance these vital skills. Marriage Encounter, for example, has taught thousands of couples the importance of regular dialogue and how to do it. Many churches offer marriage enrichment series. Our own local retreat house frequently hosts a night for married couples, including presentations about deepening marital communication.

We know, too, that when our struggles are especially painful, there is help available. Professionals trained in the dynamics and techniques of communication can be invaluable. It may require hard work, but the payoff can be a stronger, happier marriage.

Having a partner to talk to is one of our greatest joys. Most of our conversations focus on the routine, but even then our talking and listening allow us to feel connected and not alone. We find that talking and listening to each other is a special gift—a gift we give to each other generously and often. After all, we are companions on life's journey and there is ever so much we have to share. Because we want to share it fully, developing good communication skills is essential. Indeed, this requires hard work, but then again, we can't think of anything worthwhile that doesn't.

Nurturing Dialogue

1. Do I regularly talk to my spouse about our marriage and other important things affecting our life together? Does my spouse do the same?

2. Would the two of us benefit from talking more frequently, even if we have to schedule the time? Would we both be willing to do this?

3. Are there obstacles that stand in the way of better communication between the two of us? What are they? When and how might we talk about ways to remove these obstacles?

4. Where is my favorite place to talk, especially to my spouse? Where is my spouse's favorite place to talk?

5. Would I be willing to work at improving my own personal communication skills? What specifically do I need to improve? Can I admit to my spouse that I recognize this need for improvement in myself?

CHAPTER SIX

Fueling Your Friendship with Fun

■ ■ ■ ■ ■

Happy couples laugh a lot. When we interviewed them, invariably there was laughter, joking, gentle teasing, and much humor. Laughter provided a lens through which they could look at their relationship and gain some perspective; it helped them to keep from taking things too seriously.

Mary Lou, a widow who had been happily married for eighteen years, recalls how she and her husband were initially attracted to each other, in large part, because they made each other laugh. "Pat could have been a professional comedian," she says, even now with a smile. "He was so darn funny. His sense of humor was what I loved most about him. Even during our low times, when we were having problems and facing obstacles, Pat could see the humor in the situation and show me how to see it, too. Even when he became sick with cancer, he retained his ability to laugh—and to make me laugh. Every now and then I picture him laughing with God, then I laugh. See, Pat is still making me laugh."

Many couples told us that laughter, play, experiencing good times together—an overall sense of having fun with your spouse—were absolutely essential for a happy marriage.

"Boredom is the archenemy of marriage. Keep things interesting, alive, and fun, and you'll have not just a good marriage, but a great one."

"If you are too busy to have fun together, you are too busy!"

"Out of all the relationships that God invented, he meant marriage to be the most fun. The problem is that we forget this when the serious stuff comes along like bills, sick kids, and troubles with the in-laws. Couples need to remember the fun they once had together and then get back to it."

"The couple that plays together stays together."

Marriage requires hard work, but that doesn't mean it should be all work and no play. That approach, in fact, almost certainly leads to eventual turbulence. Having fun together as a couple does some important things for a marriage.

Having fun together builds friendship. Fun and laughter is a form of sharing that helps you appreciate and enjoy each other, which generates deeper intimacy. When you engage in something fun, things like residual anger or frustration seem to vanish and the slate is wiped clean so you can start fresh.

Having fun together recharges the batteries and generates new energy. At one time or another, monotony dogs the heels of most marriages; it certainly has ours. The demands of work, family, and other commitments can wear you down—wear you out. Something as simple as playing a game—cards, a board game, or cribbage, for example—after a long, exhausting day can energize and renew you. The experience of fun lifts your spirits and provides an emotional and physical boost.

Having fun together creates memories. Fun times are special times, and so it is not at all surprising that we remember these times fondly. Many of the people we talked to who had fulfilling marriages readily recalled fun-filled events with their spouses that, in some instances, had taken place over fifty years ago. Yet, these memories were vivid in their minds and cherished in their hearts.

Molly and John met at a St. Patrick's Day dance in 1939.

John: I thought she was the most beautiful girl there. We danced every dance that night, even though plenty of other men tried to cut in.

Molly: I didn't want the evening to end. I enjoyed myself like I never had before, and I also felt something in my heart I had never experienced before. Later, I knew it was love for John.

John: A year to the day we were married (*pausing to kiss Molly on the cheek*), and we've been dancing together ever since.

Having fun together can improve your sexual relationship. God intends husbands and wives to enjoy sex and have fun together sexually. For some couples this comes easily; others struggle with the notion of sex as play. The truth is, joyful sex is one of marriage's greatest gifts. If you can bring the fun-loving, playful side of yourselves to your sexual relationship, the intimate side of your marriage can be made even more enjoyable and pleasurable. Engaging in playful sex can also keep sex from becoming routine and lackluster, helping keep the excitement and romance alive and well for years to come. Needless to say, if a couple struggles with barriers that inhibit the sexual experience and keep it from being fun and fulfilling, seeking professional help can be well worth the investment of time and money.

Finding Your Own Fun

Ultimately, the two of you are the only ones who can determine what is most appealing and best for you when it comes to having fun together. Your individual experiences may in no way resemble what other couples call "fun." Just remember that fun time is anything and everything you choose to make it. Tap into that wealth of goodness as often as you can, and watch your sense of closeness grow.

We offer the following suggestions as guidelines in your pursuit of having fun together.

Spontaneous fun is often the best kind. This kind of fun is unplanned and unrehearsed; it just happens. After all, we played spontaneously as children; no one had to teach us how to have fun or plan our fun times for us. We simply knew, almost instinctively, how to have fun.

Most of us, however, have grown into adults thinking that having fun is for children, that having fun needs to get put on the back burner and completely forgotten. It is especially sad to watch couples who genuinely enjoyed having fun together before marriage but who seem to have forgotten how once they were married.

Think back to your dating days—and perhaps even further back, to your childhood. What did you do to have fun? Can you recreate some of that together?

Because children can teach us so much about being spontaneous and free-spirited, it is good for adults to spend time with them. They can teach us all over again how to let go, how to be silly, how to play, rejoice, and have fun. In this respect, children can become our wisest and best teachers, if only we allow the lesson to sink in and become part of us.

Create your own humor video library. Make a list of the funniest movies and television shows you know about, and start buying them or renting them from a video store—then arrange for special times together to enjoy them. Get your popcorn or favorite treat, curl up together on the couch, and let the fun begin. The laughter will be good for your souls and good for your marriage.

Make dating each other a lifelong practice. There is no need to relegate dating to the time before you married. It can, in fact, be an ongoing part of your marriage. Many couples characterize their dating days as being full of anticipation, fun, excitement, and surprise. Back then the goal was simply to have a good time together while getting to know each other. Those are still good goals, and the end results are well worth the effort.

Go ahead. Ask your spouse for a date—and enjoy that delicious moment when your spouse *asks you*! Have fun together and fall in love all over again.

Celebrate your anniversaries. An anniversary provides a ready-made opportunity for quality fun time. You don't have to spend a lot of money, just celebrate your special day in a special way—in ways that are meaningful to you both. Consider celebrating your wedding anniversary *every month*. If you were married on the fifteenth of the month, make the fifteenth of each month special in some small way, even if it's just a simple lunch at a fast-food restaurant or a glass of wine together in the evening followed by lovemaking. Imagine the fun just *counting* the months to see *what anniversary this one is for you*!

Consider renewing your marriage vows on your wedding anniversary each year. Just join hands and, once again, pledge your love, trust, and fidelity to each other. You don't need a priest or minister present to witness this sacred moment; the two of you can bless each other, bless your rings, and bless the life you share. Spend quiet time together reflecting on the years behind you and ahead of you. Share your disappointments, your joys, your dreams, with a special focus on the good times you've enjoyed together.

Plan a Care Day each week or several times a month. Together select a day that will be your Special Care Day, a day when you both have the right to ask each other for one reasonable favor. You might want to ask for a back rub right before bed, a late-night walk together, or even time alone just for yourself. The sky's the limit. Just be reasonable and considerate of your partner.

Couples who have a regular Care Day for their marriage look forward to these days with great anticipation. These days provide wonderful opportunities for you both to identify and respond to each other's needs—and they're fun! Try this technique for a month, and then talk about how it has affected your relationship. If you like the results, keep doing it.

Create a Fun Jar. On separate slips of paper write the fun things the two of you enjoy doing together, and put the slips of paper in a jar. Then, every now and then, perhaps at unexpected moments, reach in, pull out a slip, and go have fun!

Create a "funny memories" video. Record yourselves relating the funny stories from your life together. Most of your stories will involve the two of you, but don't forget those individual ones. Remembering the incidents and stories will not only be great fun, but what you create has the potential to become a family heirloom that generations yet unborn will someday watch with delight.

Be open to new experiences and new kinds of fun. Remain flexible and maintain a sense of adventure. Consider a weekend of back-packing in the mountains. Snakes? You're afraid of snakes? Well, they're terrified of you. Give it a try. You may have a terrific time. Or consider browsing the craft display at an art fair—you may discover a lot more than just a bunch of junk and clutter. Go together and have a good time.

Whenever possible, do fun things together that provide you opportunities to touch each other. Touching reminds you who you are and what you are all about—two lives touching, trusting, befriending each other, rejoicing together, renewing each other, growing closer ever more deeply into this gift we call marriage.

Our Personal Experience

We look at having fun together as a great stress-buster. It has long been known that fun-filled activities, especially those accompanied by lots of laughter, can refresh, relax, even heal the body and spirit. Such activities drain off dangerously high levels of stress, making them good medicine for body, mind, and spirit.

During periods when our life seems to become inundated by too many demands and too little time and energy to respond to them, we plan something fun. It may be for just a few hours, a whole day, a weekend, or a fun-filled vacation that lasts a week or more. Planning play and then carrying it out gives us something to look forward to. Somehow we feel stronger and better equipped to cope with the demands of life. Planning fun together provides us with a different perspective on our problems.

Having fun together helps us remain connected as a couple. For us, the goal of our marriage, beginning the day we exchanged our vows, has been to join our lives as fully as is humanly possible. To achieve this goal we draw upon any resource and utilize any tool available to us. Having fun together—playing, laughing, celebrating—constitutes such a tool.

We are especially conscious about having fun *with each other*. We want to avoid living out our marriage in such a way that we look for fun and fulfillment primarily with other persons. While we both have friends with whom we share fun-filled activities, our greatest and most memorable fun comes from those things we do together. Having fun together is a way for us to bond and blend our lives as we experience the pleasure of each other's company. It helps create an environment in which the love we pledged on our wedding day may grow strong and endure.

Nurturing Dialogue

1. Have we made having fun together an important part of our relationship? If not, why not?
2. What do I most enjoy doing with my spouse? What do I think my spouse most enjoys doing with me?
3. Is there something fun and exciting that I would like to do with my spouse? Can I discuss this idea with my spouse?
4. Could the two of us spontaneously do something fun and enjoyable—today? What might that be?

CHAPTER SEVEN

Anger: The Land-mine Emotion

■ ■ ■ ■ ■

In our discussions about marriage, we made it a point to ask couples about the difficult periods in their relationship. What were the most difficult times? How did they deal with those times? What did they learn from having struggled through those times together? Most of what couples shared with us centered around what we call "land-mine emotions": explosive feelings or attitudes that have the ability to do great damage to a relationship.

Carolyn, married twelve years, captures the idea behind this concept. "Remember the statement from the comic strip *Pogo:* 'We have met the enemy, and he is us'? On their wedding day, every couple should be reminded of that statement, because it is especially true in marriage." Looking back over her own marriage, Carolyn considers where the greatest challenges came from. "Generally, the greatest threat to a marriage doesn't come from outside the marriage, but from within. Each of us brings our unique emotional makeup to a relationship, and it can work for or against a couple. Believe me, if you don't learn to control your feelings, it won't be long and they will start controlling you. Then, when they decide to break loose, it's just like having a bucking bronco in your living room—and when it's all over, there's an awful lot of debris and a lot of things that will need fixing."

Although the list of land-mine emotions or attitudes includes everything from jealousy to sarcasm, the one that surfaced in almost every conversation we had with couples was *anger*. Anger seems to be the one land-mine emotion that sooner or later explodes in every marriage, often wreaking havoc and testing the couple's coping skills to the limit.

The first experience of anger in a marriage is usually threatening and frightening and, in some cases, enlightening:

"The first time Sam got mad at me, I was convinced our marriage was over—even though we had been married for only three months. I went to the bedroom and cried and cried, expecting him to walk in and tell me he was leaving. Well, he did walk in, not to tell me he was leaving but to apologize. That was thirty-seven years ago."

"I was the first one to get angry and start an argument. At the end of the blowup, Cathy said to me, 'Right now, I don't like you very much, but I will always love you.' That was a real eyeopener for me. I realized right then how committed to me she was and how lucky I was to have her for my wife. I came to appreciate her so much that since that time I have seldom started another argument. I value our marriage too much, and most of the time the issue isn't worth fighting over. So instead we turn our would-be arguments into discussions. Believe me, that's a lot more productive."

Because anger is probably the most difficult emotion for any of us to manage, it tends to take over our lives, push us around, and lead us to do and say things that, under normal circumstances, we might find repugnant or even unthinkable. Although there are times in a marriage when anger is appropriate, its impact most often tends to be negative rather than positive.

Anger: The Facts

Anger becomes especially dangerous to the marital relationship when it remains unresolved, churning beneath the surface where it becomes more toxic with time. Eventually, it is likely to be carried into the bloodstream of the relationship, where it can poison every aspect of marital interaction. We cannot begin to deal with anger constructively, however, until we understand it. Armed with some facts, a married couple is better prepared to deal with both the emotion and the issues.

Anger always comes with a message. Because the message of anger often is not clear, the challenge is to learn how to read the message and use the information. For example, since past relationships often affect present ones, you can easily—without being aware of what you're doing—transfer emotions from one relationship to another. People whose parents were emotionally unavailable during their childhood may, as adults, become enraged when their spouse seems emotionally unavailable.

Emotions, first and foremost, tell you something about *yourself.* Instead of reacting to your emotions blindly and making a bad situation even worse, listen to what your emotions are saying and allow them to teach you something about yourself. For example, anger is often the expression of fear. Acknowledge your anger with the question, "What am I afraid of in this situation?"

Anger (like all land-mine emotions) can camouflage the facts. Anger is the emotional reaction to a circumstance that is causing you pain. When someone intends to hurt you, your anger is immediate. In marriage, however, the inflicted pain is seldom intentional. This fact does not lessen the pain, of course, but it does help you view your anger from a different perspective. We human beings are prone to reading into things, misinterpreting details, making false assumptions, blowing things out of proportion, even distorting reality—and then overreacting to the feelings generated by all of these. Before you respond with anger to the feeling of being hurt, slow down and check out the facts. Doing so may stop conflict before it gets started.

Anger is not a tool to use to change a person. "If I show my spouse how mad I am about this situation, he/she will be distressed and will change his/her behavior." This seldom produces satisfactory results. The expression of anger in this kind of situation is usually interpreted as a form of attack, leaving the other spouse on the defense. This, in turn, can cause a counterattack, followed by a full-scale battle.

People change only if they want to. All too often, the experience of external pressure intended to bring about change causes only resentment—and sometimes reinforces the undesirable behavior. Compromise or negotiation is likely to be more effective.

Anger feeds on itself. Anger is a hungry emotion; it demands to be fed if it's allowed to go unresolved. We all know the experience of having been angry about something—and getting angrier and angrier with time. The issues generating anger *must* be resolved if your marriage is to find a steady and healthy course. The Bible says that we should not let the sun go down on our anger, and this is good advice. We cannot turn our emotions on and off, of course, so letting go of anger simply because it's sunset may be impossible. But we can acknowledge our anger, which is the first step toward resolving it. We can admit to ourselves and our spouse that we are angry; we can state why we are angry; and we can commit to bringing our best and rested selves to resolving that anger as soon as possible. When the sun goes down on denied or ignored anger, it's going to be there in the morning, ready to make your life miserable—another day of hurt and pain. Being honest about your anger and then working toward compromise with regard to the issues is a far better approach than letting anger feed on itself until it devours your goodness.

Dealing with Anger

It isn't possible to eliminate anger from life; it's part of the human condition. But it need not be a destructive emotion that causes repeated—and perhaps greater—pain. In fact, we can credit anger with being a powerful friend telling us something about ourselves. As long as we don't give anger control of the situation, we can deal with it in constructive ways. The following suggestions will help you deal with anger before it becomes a destructive force.

Set limits on your anger. Under the right circumstances, a tiny flame can become a roaring inferno. Don't allow your anger to become transformed into rage, where it is far more likely to do serious damage to both of you. Marriage is not a win or lose proposition. Limit your anger to the issue at hand. Going back five, ten, or twenty years and digging up old issues only adds fuel to the fire. Make your focus as specific as possible and stick to it.

Don't let your anger become an eternal flame that never goes out. Work toward a rapid resolution. There is nothing to be gained by feeding and nurturing anger, keeping it alive and well. Doing so only gives it more power. If you are not the master of your anger, you will—sooner or later—become its slave.

Touch when you're angry. Because the energy of anger doesn't exactly lend itself to being "touchy-feely," this will take a loving and conscientious effort. Once you acknowledge your anger, direct the energy that is driving your anger toward a point of gentle contact with your spouse. The power of a gentle touch can defuse the power of anger leaving both of you ready to look at the issue with a renewed commitment to resolution. In the midst of the emotional turbulence that you both experience, you literally want to stay in touch with each other. Something as simple as touching can help you feel connected, and nothing will be resolved until you're connected.

Keep the channels of communication open. When in the grip of powerful emotions, it is common not to know what to say or how to say it, or to say things you inevitably regret later. Unresolved anger usually leads to poor communication, and poor communication prevents the anger from being resolved, thus creating a vicious circle.

Many times it can be helpful to use simple "I feel" statements that provide your spouse with information about what is going on inside of you. "I feel" sad, hurt, lonely, upset, resentful, betrayed—all these communicate to your spouse a sense of what you are experiencing. This is a far better approach than attacking, insulting, or blaming your spouse, that is, engaging in negative dynamics that only serve to make a bad situation worse.

When marriages are rocked by difficult times, communication becomes even more important. The feeling of strong emotions is not a good reason to shut down the communication process.

You may need to try various—and perhaps "new"—techniques to get through your tough times, but resolving negative emotions is vital to the life of your marriage. Handling your emotions constructively, especially resolving anger, helps keep communication alive. Only with ongoing good communication will you be able to survive the emotional hurricanes that sooner or later come ashore in all marriages.

Change your perspective. While you are trying to cope with strong feelings such as anger, don't forget the love you share. After all, it is because you love each other that you feel your emotions so strongly. The person you are closest to and whom you love the most can often get under your skin the quickest and set you off in an instant. Remember the commitment you made to each other in and through your marriage vows, and your pledge to walk toward the future together. The two of you are life partners, and nothing should alter that.

Recalling your love and commitment will help you take into consideration what your spouse may be experiencing. This is not to deny or ignore your own feelings; rather, considering your spouse's perspective allows you to glimpse the fact that there is more than one way to interpret the situation. And when there is more than one way to interpret the situation, resolution comes quicker—and perhaps easier. Experiencing your own feelings and taking your spouse's perspective into consideration is crucial in keeping you from losing your way when your vision has been clouded by disturbing emotional reactions.

Learning how to handle land-mine emotions is a lifelong challenge. This does not mean that our strong emotions will forever be unbeatable foes that bully us and threaten our most valued relationships. We can acquire the personal and interpersonal skills that give us more control over these emotions and, in the process, make our marriage happier and healthier. It is definitely worth the effort, because a working knowledge of these skills can help ensure a truly fulfilling marriage.

Our Personal Experience

Early in our marriage some issue (we can't remember what it was) caused both of us to become angry. It was in that first experience of being angry with each other that we became aware of how differently each of us handles anger. Our anger had to be addressed if the problem was going to be resolved.

Susan: I was raised in a family where we verbalized our anger as soon as we felt it. We got mad, blew up, and then it was over and done with. I was surprised when Bill didn't act like that, even though I knew he was angry.

Bill: In my family, anger tended to be suppressed. When it finally did surface, it exploded with the kind of volcanic force that scared me, especially as a child. Anger was best avoided or denied, so I hid my anger, often pretending I wasn't angry when I really was seething.

Susan: I wanted Bill to tell me what he was angry about, but he only withdrew and kept it to himself—and then I felt alone and helpless. I didn't know what to do, and I didn't know how to reach him.

Bill: Fortunately, I knew that my behavior was not good for me or for our marriage. I finally asked Susan to sit down with me, and we talked about our feelings and how to avoid this situation again.

Susan: We agreed that if we became angry, we would tell the other about it right away, talk about it, and try to resolve it as quickly as possible.

Bill: Especially for me that means no distancing or withdrawing. I have to face the fact that I am angry, not let my anger scare me, and then face the issue head-on. I've discovered that we can, in fact, "teach old dogs new tricks." Although occasionally I slip up, I think I am better at identifying and acknowledging my anger and then articulating it to Susan.

Susan: We are learning together how to handle our anger, and that's been good for our marriage.

In our years of marriage, we have found that most issues are not worth all the angry energy we often put into them. We decided even before we married that we did not want a relationship characterized by constant bickering or lots of arguments over small things. It didn't take long for us to discover that most of the issues that generated anger were really pretty minor. When we feel we're getting angry, we start by asking ourselves two questions: *Is this worth getting angry over?* and *Will this matter in a week?* Most of the time the answer is "no" on both counts. Instead of jumping in with our anger, trying to hide and deny our anger, or beginning to blame and criticize the other—as if the other is supposed to "fix" things— we *admit* that we're angry, and we're clear about *why* we're angry. This approach saves our emotional energy for the truly important things of our marriage.

We like to think of this as a win-win approach to our relationship: we both "win" in some way. A basic marriage counseling principle states that the spouse who is always being asked to give in will remain angry and hostile, and healing in the relationship will most likely not take place.

When trying to resolve issues with great explosive potential, a win-win approach allows both of us to feel like we somehow came "out ahead." We look for opportunities to compromise, so each of us can come away reasonably satisfied.

A little empathy, respect, and understanding go a long way in marriage. Often, we are too quick to criticize or react negatively when our spouse displays strong emotions. Claim your own emotions. Imagine what your spouse's experience of the situation might be. Ask yourself if the effort of anger is worth the weight of the issue at hand. Recall the love and commitment that characterized your wedding day. Keep an open mind. All these simple guidelines can help you keep the land-mine emotions from bringing pain and discord to your marriage.

Nurturing Dialogue

1. What emotions are the most difficult for me to handle? What emotions are the most difficult for my spouse to handle? Can we talk to each other about these difficult emotions and why we think they're so difficult for us?
2. Do I handle my land-mine emotions better today than when I was first married? If so, to what might I attribute this?
3. What skills would I like to learn to help me handle my land-mine emotions more effectively so that my marriage will realize the benefits? How can I go about acquiring these skills?

CHAPTER EIGHT

The "Triple A" Approach to Energizing Your Marriage

■ ■ ■ ■ ■

In our quest to identify the common denominators of happy marriages, we noticed that couples used certain words more often than others. Three words in particular surfaced again and again—*acceptance*, *attitude*, and *affirmation*. We have come to refer to these as the "triple A's to energizing your marriage."

The battery known as the "triple A" is one of the smallest batteries available, yet one of these miniature powerhouse cells has kept a clock of ours running for nearly two years. In a similar fashion, when acceptance, attitude, and affirmation become realities in a marital relationship, they have a special power to energize a marriage for the long haul.

Acceptance

Life is not perfect, and thus marriage is not perfect. This was clear in all the discussions we had with couples about what made their relationships satisfying. Not one couple described their marriage as perfect.

Many couples did say, however, that they naively entered marriage expecting a near perfect state of life with an ideal partner who would surely meet their deepest needs at all times. Then, when they found themselves having to face harsh disappointments about themselves, their spouse, and their relationship, romance began to fade—painfully. What saved them from marital shipwreck was their ability to move into a new way of relating based on the *acceptance* of far more realistic perceptions and expectations.

Martha: When I married Alex twenty-nine years ago, I really did believe that he was a knight in shining armor who would fulfill all my dreams. Instead, because he was a trucker who was gone most of the time, leaving me with almost all of the responsibilities, I started to resent him. After awhile his armor began to look pretty tarnished to me.

Alex: So, when I would get back home after being away maybe a week or longer, my reception was lukewarm at best. It made me want to stay away even more.

Alex and Martha faced the same disappointment that countless newly married couples realize, sometimes within a very short time after they marry: married life is not quite what they expected. The knight in shining armor and the fair damsel most loving are real people with shortcomings. How did Alex and Martha handle this realization?

Alex: One day when it just seemed like we couldn't live that way any longer, the two of us sat down and talked and talked and talked. We agreed that my job was providing us with a good living—but it was causing us to drift apart. Instead of being afraid of Martha's anger and running from it, I accepted it as understandable. I know I wouldn't like it if she was gone for a week at a time on a regular basis. And she accepted the fact that we might have to continue living that way, at least until new opportunities were available. I promised Martha that I would begin looking for a different job close to home and, sure enough, within three months I was employed locally. That took away a lot of stress and gave us a chance to start facing and enjoying the realities of marriage.

Martha: We both changed our outlook, did some compromising, and the rest, as they say, is history—twenty-nine years of our history.

Acceptance is the first of the triple A's that helps a marriage stabilize, especially during the early years. Alex and Martha were willing to accept the fact that their marriage was not going to be the strong, intimate, lasting relationship they were both looking for given their situation. They were also willing to accept the fact that they couldn't change their situation overnight.

What else must a married couple *accept?*

Accept imperfections. No marriage is perfect, because there are no perfect human beings. Besides, perfection in a relationship is not necessary for happiness and fulfillment. In fact, many of the couples we talked with admitted their gratitude for an imperfect partner—knowing their own imperfections.

Accept your differences. No two people, in all of time and in all of creation, have ever been exactly alike. The two of you were born different—perhaps very different—and most of your differences will last a lifetime. Instead of trying to change each other, accept, respect, perhaps even celebrate your differences. When you take a close look at your differences, you may even find yourselves to be a dynamic team of complementary strengths.

Accept your problems. When one set of problems is resolved, a new set invariably crops up. Couples seldom reach a point where they feel like they have "settled everything." Some problems created by your unique personalities, by the ways you were raised, and by the mere difference between males and females may never fully be resolved. Instead of letting these problems create conflicts, strive to be more adaptable and save your energy for the really important stuff.

Accept your limitations. Each of you is a finite human being with limited gifts, abilities, intelligence, awareness, energy, and so on; neither of you is super human. Keep your personal expectations, expectations of your spouse, and expectations of your relationship within reason. You can accomplish only so much in a day, in a week, in a lifetime, and part of your responsibility as spouses is to help each other be aware of this when limits are reached. Do not overextend yourselves and invite burnout.

Attitude

There is an old saying that attitude is altitude. Indeed, whether your marriage achieves the lofty heights of deep fulfillment or barely gets off the ground seems, in large part, to be affected by the attitudes you bring to your relationship.

An *attitude* is a way of thinking, a way of viewing and interpreting people, things, and circumstances. Today, when people say, "You have an attitude," they generally mean you have a chip on your shoulder. But an attitude does not have to be negative or hostile. Rather, it can be positive and peaceful.

Unlike emotions, that seem to have a life and energy of their own at times, we can choose our attitude. If we want to be negative, cross, and argumentative, we may do so; but we are equally free to choose to be positive, pleasant, and, agreeable. Recovery programs like Alcoholics Anonymous sometimes refer to a negative attitude—sharp negativity, judgmentalism, toxic anger, and distorted ideas—as "stinkin' thinkin'." When we engage in stinkin' thinkin', we turn sour and reek of pessimism.

As soon as we wake up in the morning, we can check out our attitude. Is it the kind of attitude we want to take with us into the day? If not, right then and there we can choose an attitude that is more to our liking. We can put our energy and focus into "having an attitude" that will leave us peaceful when we turn out the lights and return to bed that night. One married woman told us,

"Marriage is ninety-five percent attitude, five percent circumstances." Imagine being able to choose ninety-five percent of the attitude that will characterize your marriage!

If we are to realize a lasting and satisfying relationship, each of us must make an honest assessment of our attitude. Ask yourself: *Is my attitude on a particular issue damaging me as well as our marriage?* If the answer is "yes," it's time to make an attitude adjustment.

Negative attitudes draw their power from dynamics such as jumping to conclusions, blowing things out of proportion, and acting as if catastrophe lurks around every corner. Abraham Lincoln said that if we look for the worst in life, we will surely find it. Dwelling on what is wrong with our marriage will make us feel discouraged and defeated, leaving us with little energy to make things better. Why not choose to dwell on what is right with our marriage? Why not feel encouraged and energized with all that is satisfying about our relationship?

What *attitudes* might you choose?

An attitude of happiness: You can choose to be happy and you can choose to have a happy marriage. It takes the simple awareness of your personal freedom to choose how you want to be. When you choose happiness and contentment, you choose to see all that is good—even great—about your marriage. Emphasize and reinforce what the two of you do well together, and build on those strengths. Find the good in even the bad situations. Make lemonade out of the lemons.

An attitude of gratitude: Count your blessings. With all its imperfections, your marriage remains a gift, and so does your spouse. Every day, let your spouse know how grateful you are that God brought the two of you together as friends and partners. Together, then, as friends, lovers, and life-partners, you can give of yourselves to others. You can give without counting the cost. After all, love isn't love until you give it away. Embracing an attitude of gratitude, you are an engine of love ready to reach out to the world.

Affirmation

Affirmation comes from a Latin word which means "to make strong." If you both consciously work at making each other strong, you will have a strong marriage.

A basic way for you to affirm your marriage is by having faith in yourselves as a couple. It does not matter what others think about your marriage; only your opinion of who and what you are matters in the long haul of a satisfying marriage. As you give each other strength and support and build your marriage together, you affirm your marriage in the best sense of the word.

"I have always been proud of my husband and my marriage," Annette says. "Always. Even when my family openly told me that they disliked Gene and didn't give us a year together. I told them I was confident it would work. I loved Gene with all my heart and soul, and I knew that he loved me in the same way. When you believe in each other, you can do anything."

"That's for sure," Gene adds with a chuckle. "And we've been believing in each other for, oh, about sixty years now."

Affirmation, of course, must be honest and straightforward. If what you say to each other is somehow phoney, you risk doing more damage than good. You can always:

Affirm each other's potential. You can be the first one "there" to support each other with encouraging words. After all, you genuinely want each other to experience success, and the two of you know best what that means. Help each other pinpoint your strengths and dream about what you might accomplish. Encourage the special skills you see in each other.

Affirm each other privately and publicly. By being sincerely complimentary you let each other know that you are proud to be together as a couple. Such affirmations also strengthen self-esteem. Affirmations are especially powerful when they are mentioned in public. In each other's company, let your family, friends, and coworkers hear you say complimentary things about your spouse. Such comments are almost a form of lovemaking.

Affirm each other with positive feedback. Coach instead of criticize. It's been said that a person who is criticized never forgets—and there is much truth to that—but criticism often evokes an angry response. Coaching, on the other hand, is nonthreatening. Affirm what went right in a given situation, but be willing to offer and receive comments about how details may have been handled in ways that would have made the situation better. Avoid putting each other on the defensive; offer positive feedback so you can focus on problem solving.

Our Personal Experience

In our own marriage, we realize that acceptance of growth and change is essential. After all, nothing and no one truly stay the same. To be alive is to change. Each of us is changing constantly, often in subtle but nonetheless significant ways. Knowing that growth and change are not threatening, we try to comment on things when we sense something is different. We welcome these comments because they are the seedlings of growth. We strive to be open and flexible so that, over the years, we find ourselves growing together rather than apart.

We're also aware of how our attitudes affect our relationship, especially when we face thorny problems. A friend of ours has underscored this approach with a funny and insightful observation: When King Saul saw Goliath, he thought, "Wow, he's too big to kill!" When David saw Goliath, he thought, "Wow, he's too big to miss!" When we bring an attitude of optimism to our relationship, everything seems to stay in proper perspective.

When it comes to affirmation, we like to think of ourselves as practicing the "ministry of encouragement." We feel that this is one of the most important things we do for each other. At every opportunity, especially when one of us feels down and discouraged, we try to boost the other's spirits. Perhaps the best way we do this is simply by making ourselves available, being willing to listen deeply, and being as understanding as possible. Our experience has been that encouragement gives rise to hope, and hope heals.

When we marry, we truly want to live happily ever after—and that doesn't have to remain the closing line from a fairy tale. We can, in fact, be deeply happy for a lifetime. Acceptance, attitude, and affirmation—the triple A's—play a big part in nurturing the special relationship that is marriage.

Nurturing Dialogue

1. Are the triple A's—acceptance, attitude, and affirmation—present in our marriage? Can I think of examples of how we practice each?
2. What has been the easiest thing I've had to accept since we married? What has been the most difficult thing I've had to accept since we married?
3. Since our wedding day, in what area has my attitude changed and become more positive? more negative? What about my spouse?
4. In what area do I think my spouse would say that I am most affirming? In what area does my spouse seem to be the most affirming toward me?
5. How would I describe the present energy level of our marriage? Is there some area of our marriage that needs revitalizing? If so, how can the two of us make that happen?

CHAPTER NINE

Healing Hurts through Forgiveness

■ ■ ■ ■ ■

When we told people about this book and invited their input about what we should include, the one theme that surfaced more than any other was the necessity of forgiveness. We heard:

"If you don't know how to forgive, you won't stay married."

"When things go wrong, it's forgiveness that repairs the hurts and makes things right again."

"Forgiveness in a marriage is just like having brakes on a car; forgiveness stops things before they get started."

Ted, a marriage counselor, has been happily married for thirty-six years. He had this to say about the power of forgiveness: "Often, when troubled couples come to me for help, I ask each of them, 'Do you have a forgiving heart?' If either answers 'no,' I know that the marriage is in serious trouble and there may be very little I can do to help turn things around."

Ted emphasizes the healing dimensions of forgiveness: "It is very difficult for deep and lasting healing to take place without forgiveness. Lack of forgiveness allows the core problems to keep repeating themselves. Each time this happens, the marital relationship suffers a little more, until finally it is overwhelmed. That is why I believe that for a successful marriage, forgiveness is not an option or a luxury. It is a necessity."

Forgiveness is one of those all-important qualities that enables a marriage to last quantitatively and qualitatively, and yet it is something with which many spouses have great difficulty. It seems we tend to misinterpret and misunderstand exactly what forgiveness is and what it can do to and for a marriage.

For example, there are those who think that to be forgiving is to be weak and wimpish, that forgiveness more or less lets the offending person "off the hook" and encourages bad behavior. These people often endorse the attitude "Don't get mad, get even."

Paula describes how this approach made her marriage—her entire life—miserable. "When my husband committed adultery and I learned about it, I was determined not to forgive him as long as I lived. I didn't want a divorce, but I did want to punish him so badly I could taste it. I wanted him to feel some of my pain, and I figured that by not forgiving him and constantly reminding him of how he had failed me, himself, and our family, I could get back at him good. I even went so far as to tell our children what he had done, adding to his humiliation.

"With time, I came close to not only destroying him but also destroying myself," she adds. "From hindsight I realize now that my sin of hatred against him was far greater than his sin of adultery. I jeopardized my own spiritual life by nurturing a spirit of unforgiveness toward him."

What turned things around for Paula and her family?

"A Sunday homily. Our pastor happened to preach on forgiveness and the gracious mercy of God, who gives us not only a second chance, but a third, fourth, and fifth chance—as many as we want. The priest also pointed out that whatever we are unable to forgive comes to control and enslave us, so in the end we become the victims of our own unwillingness to forgive.

"As I listened to him, I knew in my heart he was right. That very day I told my husband that I forgave him. I asked his forgiveness for the ways I had hurt him, and we started over. That was fifteen years ago. My husband is deceased now, but the years we had together after our reconciliation were good. Healing really did take place, and we were both glad that our marriage survived."

Without forgiveness, restoring a badly damaged marriage is next to impossible. With forgiveness, even a badly injured marriage can be saved, healed, and renewed. In even the closest human relationships, including the best of marriages, human beings disappoint, hurt, fail, and wound one another—sometimes without even realizing what they have done. Only forgiveness can repair the damage.

Forgiveness is the act of acknowledging, perhaps only to ourselves, that we have been wronged, yet we deliberately choose to let go of the desire to get even. Like many people, husbands and wives often get confused about forgiveness, because they believe it has to be a *feeling*. If they don't *feel* forgiving, they must not have forgiven. But forgiveness is much more than a feeling. It's a choice, lived out day by day. Feelings, after all, change; we may feel forgiving one day but not the next. Genuine forgiveness, however, is an act of the will.

The old saying that feelings are not facts can be particularly true in this respect. The recurrence of unforgiving feelings after we make a choice to forgive our spouse does not mean we have not forgiven. Rather, it may mean that we have to reaffirm our choice, that we have to continue with the *process* of forgiveness, which often goes beyond a one-time decision.

Forgiveness Is Not...

Forgiveness does not mean that we condone our spouse's behavior, especially if it was inappropriate or truly wrong. Jesus gives us an example with the woman who was about to be stoned for the act of adultery (see John 8:1-11). When he says, "Go your way, and from now on do not sin again," he was very clear about not condoning her behavior—yet he was very clear about forgiveness.

Forgiveness is not a form of absolution; a person is still

responsible for what was done. Forgiveness, in fact, is often the critical element that allows a person to take the appropriate steps to make necessary amends.

The act of forgiving does not mean that we are entitled to play the role of martyr ("Look at how much you have made me suffer!"); self-righteousness is not part of forgiveness. Nor does it mean that we will never get angry if the behavior is repeated. In fact, a statement of genuine forgiveness is very clear that pain and anger will, indeed, be experienced if the behavior is repeated.

Forgiveness is sometimes confused with mercy, but strictly speaking, mercy means a *reduced sentence*. Forgiveness is not conditional. Forgiveness for a particular act is without limits. We do not forgive "if"; we simply forgive. It also does not mean putting our spouse on probation ("I'll be watching to see if you slip up"). Rather, forgiveness is our deliberate choice to wipe the slate clean. It is a way of saying, "I will never bring up this incident again."

The Litmus Test of Forgiveness

We have to be careful when we forgive. After all, when we experience pain, we have a tendency to do things that will help alleviate some of the hurt. It's quite possible for us to think of ourselves as forgiving when all we're doing is trying to make ourselves feel better.

Two telltale signs that we really have not forgiven our spouse are sarcasm and resentment. Sarcasm comes from two Greek words that mean "to cut the flesh," and it is just that in marriage. When we are sarcastic with our spouse, we are simply using a verbal cleaver to slice and dice his or her character. Sarcasm is a sure sign that we are still angry and that we are allowing our anger to contaminate the way we communicate. We have not yet let go of the hurt—and thus we are not forgiving.

Resentment, too, clouds true forgiveness. Resentment comes from feeling that our spouse has not sufficiently atoned for the wrong.

She or he owes us something more, and we will not relinquish the negative feelings until the debt is settled in full. Unfortunately, of course, our spouse may never atone or "pay back in full" what we think our due is. If we find ourselves nursing resentment, we are not ready to forgive.

Why Forgiveness Is Critical

No marriage is without those incidents that call for forgiveness. No matter how compatible and satisfying the relationship is, there will be those times when pain and disappointment occur because of a hurt one spouse caused another.

Forgiveness is crucial in a marriage because:

God expects us to have forgiving hearts. The Scriptures overflow with God's extravagant forgiveness. Because we have been forgiven by God, we, too, are to forgive. In no human relationship is this more critical than in marriage.

Many times your spouse may hurt you deeply and never even realize it. A careless remark, an act of neglect, some inconsiderate act, or an insensitive attitude can cause you to seethe with anger. In some of these instances, you can forgive without your spouse knowing he or she has been forgiven.

We forgive, then, because without forgiveness both our spiritual journey with our spouse and our relationship with God as our unseen Third Partner in the marriage can suffer greatly. Forgiveness thus becomes not only the right thing to do, but sometimes the only thing to do.

Forgiveness allows a marriage to move on. The feelings of anger and resentment that come with being hurt have a way of immobilizing a marital relationship. It can grind to a halt and get stuck as the couple wallow in a mire of negativity.

Forgiveness provides you the freedom to move forward once

again. It liberates both you and your spouse from being held captive by toxic emotions.

Forgiveness challenges you to growth and maturity. Genuine forgiveness does more than end a rift: it compels both of you to stretch yourselves emotionally and spiritually, to become more than what you have been to this point in time. Forgiveness changes you—for the better. To forgive and to be the recipient of forgiveness serve as catalysts for achieving your full potential as human beings, as children of God, as lifelong committed partners.

Forgiveness teaches you the real meaning of love. Forgiveness is linked to love because it involves your best self. Forgiveness desires the highest good for the person forgiving and the one being forgiven. You cannot love unconditionally without being able to forgive unconditionally. Forgiveness is transformative; it changes cold hearts into hearts on fire with compassion and concern, so that you come to learn the true meaning behind Christ's words: "Love one another as I have loved you" (see John 15:12).

Practicing forgiveness is role modeling at its best. When you turn your fights into guerilla wars that seem to go on indefinitely, you are teaching your children to fight in the same way. On the other hand, when you choose to be forgiving and when you value reconciliation, you show your children and other family members an alternative to conflict and dysfunctional behavior. When you model forgiveness you influence generations yet to come with the healing legacy that comes from being a forgiving family.

Self-forgiveness

Many of the couples we interviewed stressed the importance of self-forgiveness, noting that people often torture themselves for years because of real or imagined sins, failings, mistakes, or simple errors in judgment. People may forgive others, including their spouse, yet refuse to forgive themselves. This can be a serious detriment to a marriage.

Refusing to forgive ourselves is a form of self-punishment that deprives us of our own compassion. Without self-forgiveness we cannot find inner peace and the healing we need after "messing up"—whatever that may have been.

Forgiving ourselves is a sign of healthy self-love. When we forgive ourselves, we chose to love ourselves as God has instructed. Resolving feelings of anger and bitterness toward ourselves is important for our own emotional and spiritual health and for the health of our marriage as well. The stability of any marriage depends in large part on the stability of both partners.

Spouses who are plagued by the inner turmoil that comes from failing to forgive and accept themselves should take steps that will lead them to healing and a renewed sense of wholeness. For some persons, this may mean spiritual counseling; others may want to pursue therapy. It is well worth the investment of time and money to work through thorny personal issues to achieve a deeper sense of freedom and happiness.

Our Personal Experience

In our own marriage, we have found that certain forms of ritual help us express and receive forgiveness, and thus heal and grow.

For example, a genuine statement of "I'm sorry," followed by a kiss, will be enough. At other times, we might just offer our hand as a gesture of reconciliation. We also find that praying together, especially the Lord's Prayer, emphasizes our willingness to forgive and be forgiven.

Writing is also effective. If something serious has damaged our sense of closeness as a couple, we turn to the visual word. We write down the hurt on a piece of paper and then together burn it in some way, letting the flame represent the healing light of Christ and the need to keep the flame of love alive in our marriage.

Ritualizing forgiveness is limited only by our creativity. We can blend words with specific activities that help us release and remove the emotional burdens we have been carrying and allow a fresh transfusion of life and energy into our marriage. In all relationships, particularly marriage, asking for and accepting forgiveness can be difficult. Yet, seeking forgiveness and bestowing forgiveness in a damaged marriage is critical to healing. Forgiveness allows us to love again, trust again, and move forward on the road of life as friends and lovers.

By draining off the sometimes toxic feelings of anger and guilt, forgiveness renews and re-energizes a marriage. Of these nine ways to nurture your marriage, forgiveness is perhaps the one thing married couples need to understand and practice most often, for in the turmoil that sooner or later assails every marriage, forgiveness is the key to peace and healing.

Nurturing Dialogue

1. Do I have a forgiving heart? Does my spouse have a forgiving heart?
2. Is forgiveness something we practice in our marriage? If not, why not?
3. Have we modeled forgiveness for our family? Have our children and/or other family members learned forgiveness by the example we offer in our marriage?
4. Knowing that forgiveness is not a feeling, how might I offer or receive forgiveness in the future?
5. After hurting each other, what kind of ritual might we create together to help us forgive and heal?

Final Thoughts

■ ■ ■ ■ ■

Contrary to the popular sentiment, marriages are not made in heaven. Rather, lasting and satisfying marriages are built by imperfect and finite human beings, little by little, day by day, here on Earth.

Those who are married—newlyweds as well as those married for many decades—know that we can always do something more, try a little harder, stretch ourselves a little farther, to improve the quality of our marriage. Positive changes in a marriage will not happen unless we want them, will them, and work for them.

We sincerely hope that these nine ways to nurture your marriage will in some way enrich your marriage. It's been said that a wedding lasts only one day, but a marriage lasts a lifetime. May you know newlywed joy throughout your lifetime together.

We wish you well.